Manifesting
Your Dream Year

Welcome to a **transformative journey** into the realms of **manifestation**, **mindfulness**, and the power of **visualization**! As we step into 2025, this book is designed to guide you in harnessing your inner potential to create the life you've always dreamed of.

Mindfulness plays a crucial role in your journey. By visualizing, you will learn to release limiting beliefs and self-doubt that may have held you back in the past. Embracing mindfulness will empower you to **achieve all your dreams!**

Are you ready to delve into the inspiring world of vision boards? This creative tool serves not only as a visual representation of your aspirations but also as a daily reminder of your goals. With this clip art book, you can craft a vision board that truly reflects your desires for 2025, turning abstract concepts into tangible realities.

Join us as we embark on this empowering adventure, helping you manifest your dreams and intentions for the coming year. The life you envision is within your reach—**let's make it happen!**

#TAKE CARE OF YOURSELF

MIND
BODY
SOUL
SPIRIT

NEW AND OLD YEAR REFLECTIONS

GRATITUDE · LESSONS LEARNED · ACHIEVEMENTS · TRADITION · LETTING GO · MINDFUL PRACTICES · REFLECTION PROMPTS · BALANCE · INTENTIONS · VALUES

Mind
Body
Soul

Health is the best Wealth.

WHEN YOU GET TIRED LEARN TO REST NOT TO QUIT

SELF CARE

Have a cup of positiviTEA

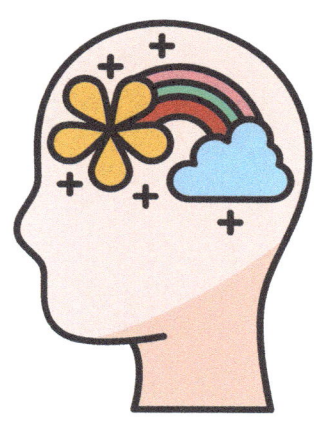

START YOUR DAY WITH POSITIVE AFFIRMATION

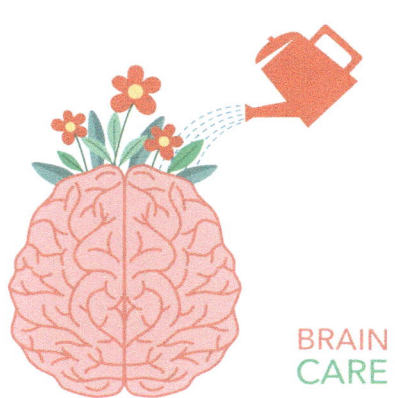

BRAIN
CARE

VACATION
IS A
STATE OF
MIND

EACH DAY
IS A FRESH
START

BE KIND
TO YOUR
MIND

GOOD
THINGS
TAKE
TIME

Be the best version
of yourself

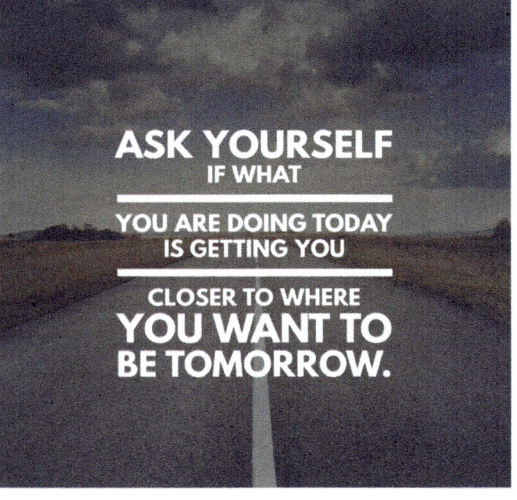

ASK YOURSELF
IF WHAT
YOU ARE DOING TODAY
IS GETTING YOU
CLOSER TO WHERE
YOU WANT TO
BE TOMORROW.

sorry, i'm too busy
manifesting

you are
made of
magic

the best is
yet to come

unstoppable
unstoppable
unstoppable

wealthy
healthy
HAPPY

my time
to shine

the best is
yet to come

wealthy
healthy
HAPPY

my time
to shine

you are
made of
magic

i deserve
GOOD
things

i deserve
GOOD
things

unstoppable
unstoppable
unstoppable

sorry, i'm too busy
manifesting

plan your day

NO BAD
vibes

I LOVE MONEY AND MONEY LOVES ME

3639

DATE _____

PAY TO THE
ORDER OF _____ $ [   ]

_____ DOLLARS 🔒

MEMO _____ _____

⑆161914353⑆ 454833⑈ 6538 92

3639

DATE _____

PAY TO THE
ORDER OF _____ $ [   ]

_____ DOLLARS 🔒

MEMO _____ _____

⑆161914353⑆ 454833⑈ 6538 92

3639

DATE _____

PAY TO THE
ORDER OF _____ $ [   ]

_____ DOLLARS 🔒

MEMO _____ _____

⑆161914353⑆ 454833⑈ 6538 92

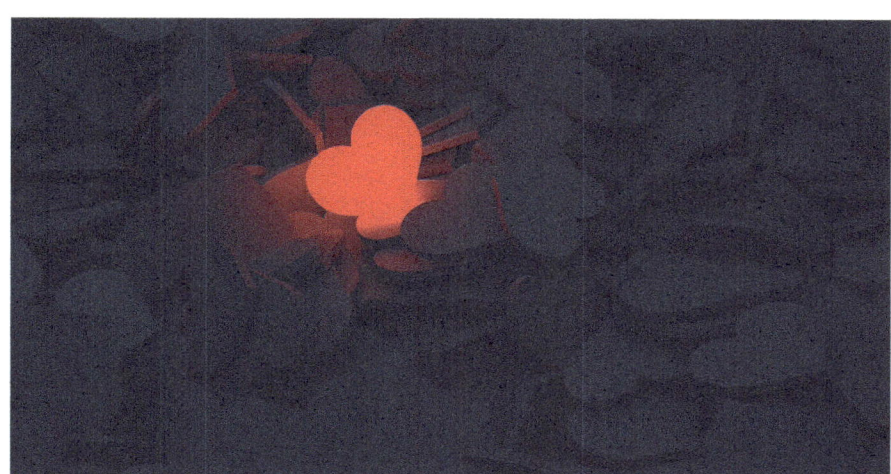

you are my

everything

love.

love·able /ˈləvəb(ə)l/ a
qualities to attract love an
love /lʌv/ *n.* A strong s
profound feeling for anot
to have a passionate a
someone, to be in love.

you brighten my day

i am
grateful

I Love you!

BE MY
VALENTINE?
☐ Yes ☐ No

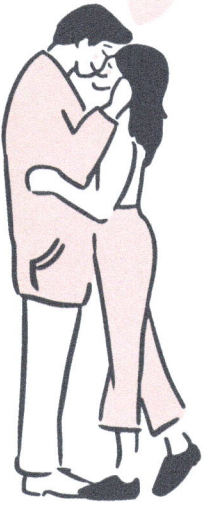

FOREVER MINE

You & Me

Happy Valentine's Day

LOVE COUPON
LOVE COUPON
YOUR WISH
LOVE COUPON • LOVE COUPON • LOVE COUPON
LOVE COUPON • LOVE COUPON

LOVE YOU

LOVE COUPON
LOVE COUPON
YOUR WISH
LOVE COUPON • LOVE COUPON

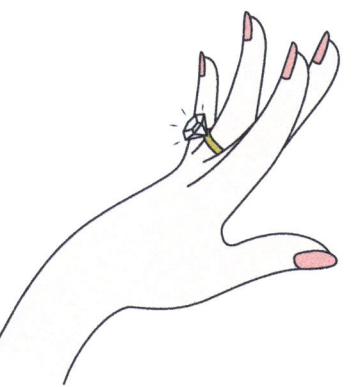

Our First Home

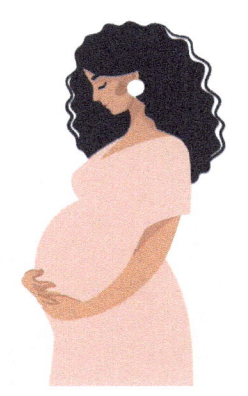

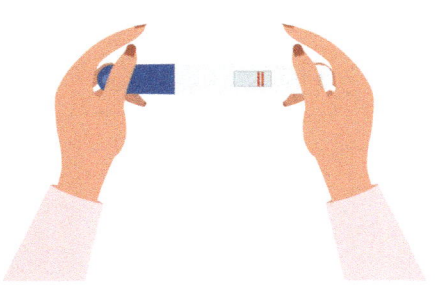

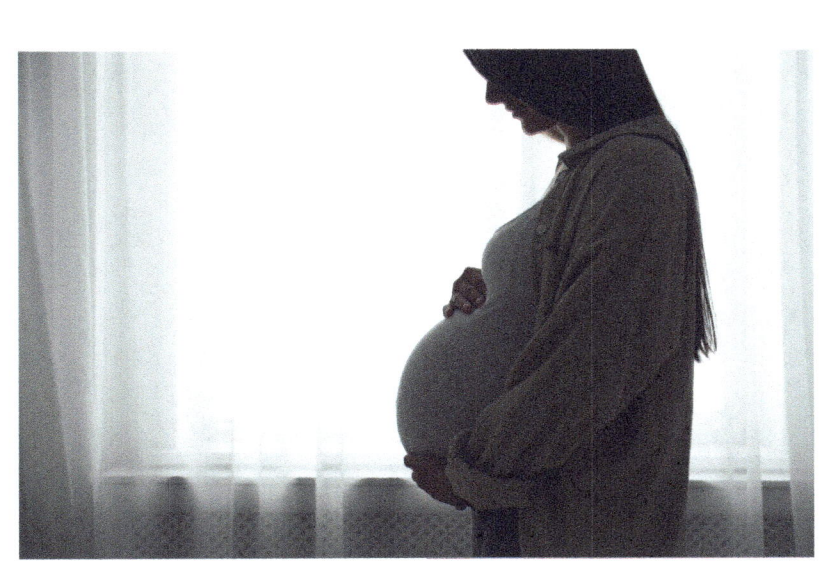
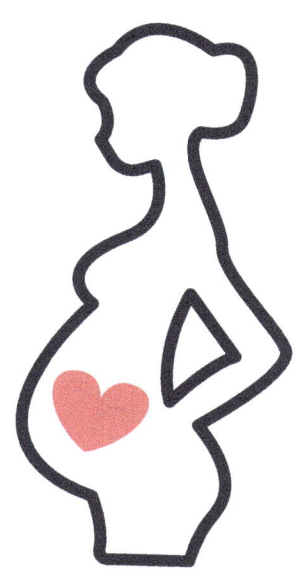

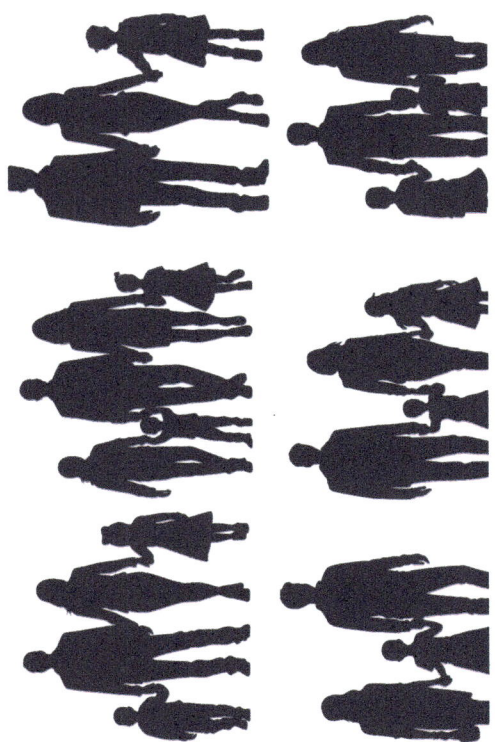

RAISE *your* VIBRATION

You ARE YOUR *own* POWER

Boost YOUR *creative* POWER WITH *magic*

EMBRACING YOUR INNER

WITCH

THE LOVERS

✦ THE MAGICIAN ✦

✦ WHEEL OF FORTUNE ✦

THE FOOL

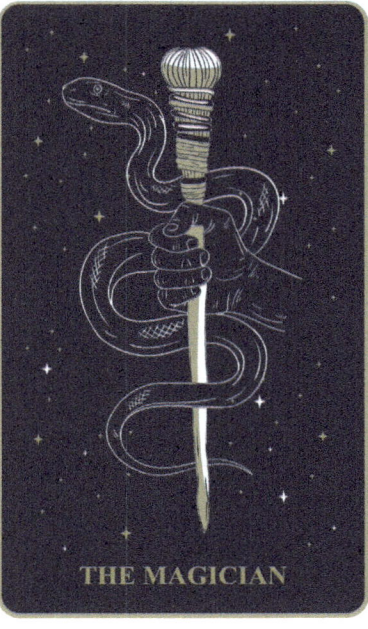

THE MAGICIAN

THE HIGH PRIESTESS

DEPARTURE ✈

HONG KONG
NEW YORK
LONDON

ARRIVALS ✈

PARIS
TOKYO
DUBAI

A B C D E F G H I J K L M N O P Q R S T
U V W X Y Z 0 1 2 3 4 5 6 7 8 9 : ? ! .

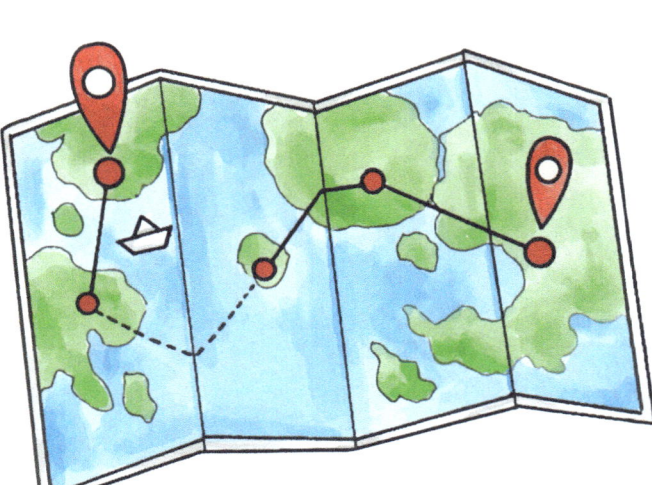

✈ Airlines

Name:

To:

From:

Date:

Flight:

Time:

Seat:

✈ Airlines

👤 Name:

📍 From: To:

🕐 Date: Time:

✈ Flight:

📌 Seat:

🎫 Boarding:

🎫 Gate:

unlock your potential

ABUNDANCE MINDSET

DIVINE FEMININE ENERGY

MY DREAMS ARE COMING TRUE

CREATE YOUR DREAM LIFE

BLESSED

I MANIFEST EVERYTHING I WANT

TRUST THE UNIVERSE

TRUST YOUR INTUITION

TRUST THE PROCESS

It is ok for me
to have everything
I want.

GRATEFUL FOR
where I am
EXCITED ABOUT
where I am going

THE MIRACLE
IS BIG ENOUGH
TO CHANGE YOUR
entire life.

I can easily afford
all that I desire.

I AM FINANCIALLY
ABUNDANT

I AM GRATEFUL
TO BE WEALTHY.

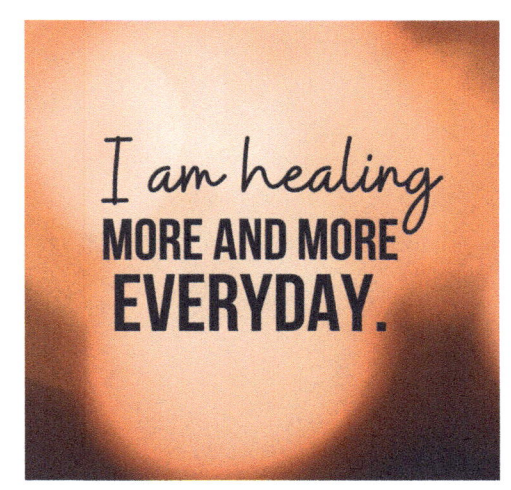

Thank you FOR THE MILLIONS OF DOLLARS THAT ARE COMING TO ME.

I am healing MORE AND MORE EVERYDAY.

I Can Do This

I'm so grateful to be alive

I have the Power to Create Change

Today is a great day

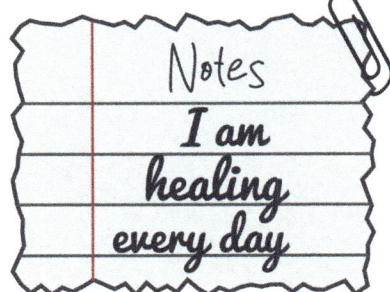

Notes
I am healing every day

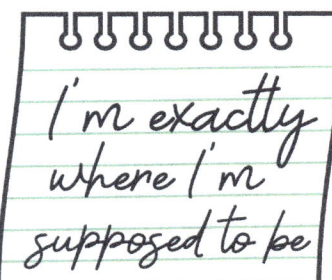

I'm exactly where I'm supposed to be

Notes
I am fearless

I'm doing the very best I can

I AM LOVED

TO GO

DRIVER LICENSE

BODY GOALS

GYM

SORE TODAY STRONG TOMORROW

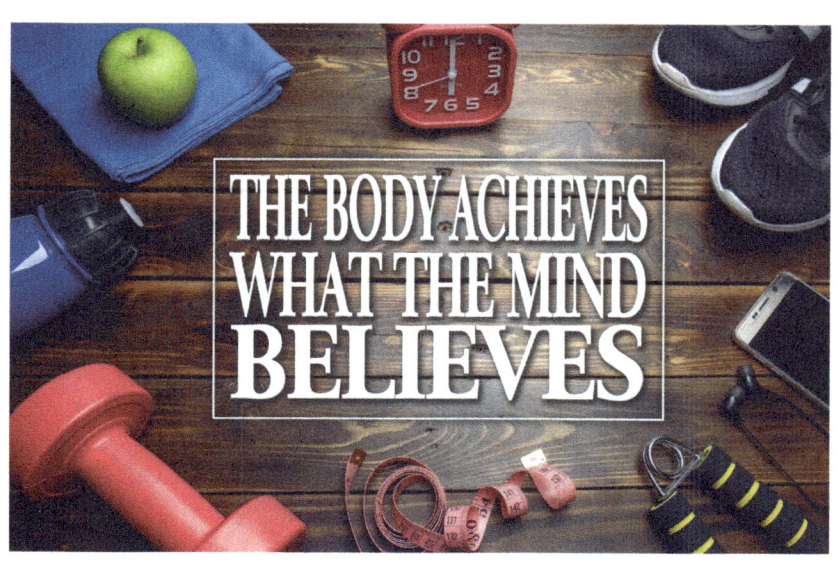

THE BODY ACHIEVES WHAT THE MIND BELIEVES

Fitness

Be HEALTHY eat HEALTHY

DRINK MORE WATER

STAY ACTIVE

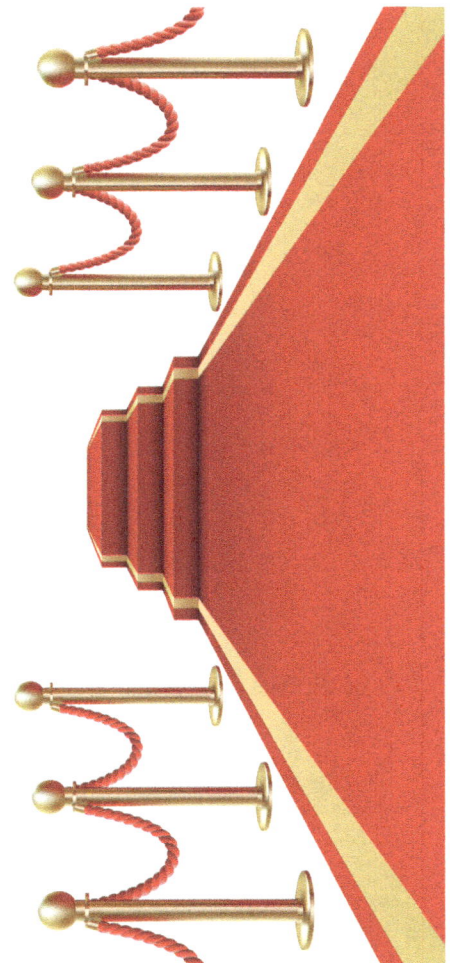

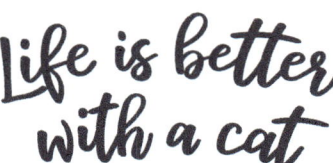
Life is better with a cat

CAT mother

HOME IS WHERE MY dog IS

I ♥ YOU!

My Favorite People Have Paws

Made in United States
North Haven, CT
08 May 2025

68685685R00052